Scratchings

A poetry collection

by

Omar C. Dylan

Dedicated to the soul of Mohamed Choukri,
the madman of the roses.

And my thanks goes to Guerbouza.

Contents

Introduction

This book is the fruit of my first navigation into the vast sea of poetry. I have always been a bookworm. My reading obsession never ceased to take me from one field to another, from Arabic literature to Chinese folklore, from fiction to cooking!

I have tasted from each and every plate, yet poetry was out of my interest. That was the case until the last 5 months. A few years ago, a dear friend had sent me a book of poetry by the outrageous writer Charles Bukowski. The book remained untouched for a couple of years. Now, as a diehard fan of Mr. Chinaski, I feel regret that I didn't pay much attention to that book. But once I started reading it, a lot has changed and, without exaggeration, I can say that his poetry was the push that threw me into this field.

The process of turning my thoughts and

feelings into poetry is strange. First of all, I
never write on paper. I don't have a notebook.
I wrote most of my poems with the help of my
phone. The second thing I would love for you
to know before you start reading is that I
wrote most of the poems while driving my car
or while working. A few of them, I have to
confess, were written in the bathroom.
Nothing can compare with the pleasure of
shitting and writing poetry.

This collection contains over 90 poems.
They talk about love, sadness, whiskey, dope,
and so many other topics. Some talk about
me, but most of them talk about everything
and nothing. I started this collection with a
poem called The fool, to introduce myself to
my readers, and I ended it with a poem called
Hope, in the hope to write more and more in
the coming years.

With love,
O.C.D.
February 10, 2019

Note from the author

The proceeds from the sale of this book will be going towards the purchase of books and school supplies as a gift to the pupils in my village.

I am a naked poem
Read me not with your eyes
But with your drunk souls

The fool

I'm a drunken fool
I circle the world
with a red balloon
I have a silly dog
and a blind kangaroo
I play the saxophone
and live on the moon

27 vodka shots

Be weird! Your life is just a joke,
a stroke of luck from a stupid dice player.
Your life and death are less important than
a chaotic red dot in the left side of a 3.8
billion years old painting.

Be insane! Wipe your ass with the Times,
masturbate while you watch Fox News.
Eat the cockroach and drink the camel piss.

Be a jerk! Sleep with Venus
and get a blow job from Aphrodite.

Be odd! Love your dog and kill the gods.
Read Bukowski and skip Rumi.
Walk fast and sleep long.
Get high and dance naked
in the dark side of the moon.

Be strange to yourself
be the God of your life
be the love to your heart
be the bullet of your head
be the soil to your feet
and the death of your greed.

Yellow chalk on the wall

I write to you
pages of my lost years
baffled
between the absent present
and the distant past.

I write to you
my thoughts burn out
in my mind
and the smoke comes out
from my ears and mouth.
The cloud weeps over my head
and the flower blooms inside my heart.

I write to you
my words turn into chaos
into fictional stories.
Turns into a trifling joke
without meaning
without taste.

I write to you
like an adult
would do
but your love taught me
to remain a child
and just let it go.

I write your name
this time on the wall
with a yellow chalk
and sit there
watching the drops of rain
dissolving your four letters name.

.

Hashish

Like a wild beast
my soul has risen
from the ruins
of my ashes
and flushed like
a glowing arrow.
Fresh
as the morning breeze.
Immortal
as the morning kiss.

Have I ever told you that...

The moon got drunk
and missed the show
that starless Saturday night
while I was freezing
on the park bench.
Circles of smoke
around my head
heaps of ashes
at my feet
writing a Merry Christmas
postcard to you.

Happy Monday, Pussy

And so the show time came to the end.
The sky brought its curtains down
the stars called it a night
the moon fell into the deep ocean
and I was left alone in the bare stage.
So I walked to the kitchen.
I was drunk or maybe not
I don't remember, but I walked.
I picked up another beer
I peered through the open window
the stars were still asleep
and the moon was beyond the horizon.
The quietness of the night was dense.
I could hear the sound of my thoughts
and the beats of my heart.
I came back to my room.
It was dark and empty
except for a pair of dirty socks,
a can of sardines, a candle, a typewriter
and Pussy.

Pussy was my cat.
She was lying on the couch.
I could see in her eyes that she was tired.
Tired of me, tired of being a cat, a pussy.
What's up, Pussy, wanna drink?
I teased her but she gave me a paw.
She curses me often and it made me laugh.
I laughed again and raised my beer.
Happy Monday, Pussy!

Necessity

Sometimes a memory needs a memory.
Your identity is engraved in your history
do not lose it.

Sometimes a face needs a mask.
Your honesty is all we ask
do not scorn it.

Sometimes a heart needs a mind.
Your love is a mirage land
do not trust it.

Silence

Your silence speaks words
like no other words
and breaks through my skin
every time you move your lips.

Your silence my lady
is magic.
Turns my red blood into green
and my tears into a diamond pearl.

Your silence is like a winged horse.
At night it takes me for a journey
to the wonderland
where you and I
dance naked beneath the starry sky.

On beauty

Dostoevsky
once said,
"Beauty will
save the
world".
I look around
I see
a choked city.
I look up
I see
a shredded sky.
I look down
I see
a deserted field.
Well,
beauty, my friend,
is the missing ring
in the chain of
the dazzling failures
of this human circus.

After all, the world
needs beauty
to save
it.

Charles' Bar Blues

Hey darlin', you wanna
know the truth of it?
I ain't a rockstar
I'm just a sidewalk flower.
Come and meet me,
babe!
Come and kiss me,
babe!
Today or the day after
in La Liberte Square.
And just to make it clear
I have been clean
for 2 months so far
but we can have a beer
like in ol' days my dear
in Charles' Bar.

Art

Drinking wine
at the funeral of your ex
is art.
Sleeping until noon
on your wedding day
is art.
Chasing a hooker
in the streets of Mecca
is art.
Shooting your brains out
at Sabbath service
is art.
Art is a sweet little demon
a feather tickling
the ears of
sleeping gods.

Inspiration

From the depth of the sea
a sound called
and as the wind blew
a wave appeared
mixed with fear and joy.
My soul stretched.
"Come to me, bohemian sailor"
beyond the divine horizon
my mermaid sadly waved.

atiloL

She was
pure and
fragile
like a
precious
Chinese
vase
and her
innocent
naked
skin
smelled
like
the soil
after
the first
rain.

Romance with a missing tooth

"So I heard that you are a writer?"
I nodded, "Yeah."
"What do you write?"
she asked again.
"Poetry. Cheap poetry ." I said.
She nodded. "Huh!
and in your free time
how do you keep yourself busy?"
she asked.

I put my arms on the table
and crossed them.
I took a deep breath
and I smiled until she could notice
my missing tooth:
"I ...
(then I looked away where
a stray dog was licking his balls)
.... recycle stories while
rolling joints."

When I turned my face
she looked as serious as Stalin
without a mustache of course.
"Do you want another drink?"
I asked.
"No. I gotta go."
And she
left.

Love is a ghost bitch

Your love
haunts me
every night
when I try to
close my eyes
and dream.
It grabs me
by the hair
and sweeps me
off my feet
'till my heart
falls out and
smashes into
blazing pieces.
Then your love
turns into a dog,
a dog from hell
raising his left leg
by a nameless
tombstone

and pisses on me
to put out
the fire
of my
low desire.

Sinner's prayer

Let's sin
brothers and sisters.
Let's sink in our lustful
dreams.
Let all the
Imams
Mullahs
Priests
and Rabbis
let them all
watch us
while we touch
we kiss
we suck.
While we make love
in the craziest ways
that the gods have
forgotten about.
Amen.

Dirty old boots

Me and my dirty old boots
walked down so many roads
and knocked on a thousand doors
'till we found yours.
So light the candles and bring the booze
'cause tonight I'm gonna play the blues
for you and my dirty old boots.

Memories

When I miss your hug
I think about the smell
of cigarettes on your coat.

When I miss your kiss
I think about the taste
of coffee on your tongue.

When I miss your touch
I think about the way
your hands squeeze my butt.

And when I think about
how much I love you
my eyes shed a tear
only for you.

Reborn under your feet

Tonight, when you close
your black smoky eyes
I will bury my blue heart
underneath your feet
and swallow the pain
'till my bloodshot eyes
rain tears
and water the dying heart.

At dawn, when the birds whistle
and the cold breeze
kisses the wet soil
my heart's bud will bloom
into a jasmine
and wait for your slender hands
to pick it up and smell
its morning perfume.

When I smoke way toooooo much weed

I often dream of
a giant white rabbit
sitting on my bed
blindfolded carrying
a frameless mirror
that reflects a black shaggy ghost
crawling on mud
and howling like a raging wolf.

Wake the fuck up
Sleepyhead!

Wake up...

Lunes

Monday showed up
on my door
glorified
like a German knight
carrying pride
upon his shoulders
on the day of his wedding
to a weary Spanish princess.

After midnight

Everyday
after midnight
I hear the echo
of your voice
in my backyard.
Sorrowed
I walk
to the graveyard
my back curved
with the burden
of the haunting
memories.
Numbed
I stop by your tombstone.
I read your name
a thousand times.
I lay next to you.
I gaze at the dark sky
and like every night,
I hear my saxophone

playing your
favorite song
to the full moon.

Obedience

My love is a Pharaonic cat.
The gods blessed her
and men feared her.
Neither a god nor a man,
a servant dog, I just worshiped her.

The sailor

Tonight
when the sailors join their cabins
I will take my boat and sail away
to the end of the ocean
rowing and drinking
to fill up a tired soul
left empty like a drum.

And tomorrow at dawn
I will dock the boat
and bury my last hope
deep underneath the soil
with no one as a witness of my sin
except for a black headed gull
hovering in the bright red sky.

iMask therefore I am

Life is a ridiculous circus
where men hide behind women
and women hide behind masks
and masks hide behind other masks.
It's not a life unless you wear a mask.
You need a mask when you wake up in the
morning
before you wash your face
and look at the broken mirror
in your dirty bathroom.
You need a mask when you have breakfast
with your babbler wife
and a double mask when you kiss her before
you leave the house.
You need a brand new mask when you go to
work.
The mask that pleases your greedy boss
and the angry clients at your office.
And when they leave, you need the mask you
brought with you from the late evening party

yesterday and wear it when
the sexy clerk sits on your lap.
Life is an endless scene of flickering cliche
and deja vu.
Cold as a beer on a hot summer night.
And only when death comes to you
like a plate of spaghetti served
by an elegant waiter in Firenze
only then you will realize how serious
death is.
Plain and simple
unmasked
like a spaghetti.

Little drops of poison

She embraces
the souvenir spheres
and swallows
the drops of poison.
Shit happens
but life goes on
and on and on
while she is burning
in the hell of patience
every other second
and reborn.

Ugly truth

After a cesarean section
a lie was born
and given
the name of
Truth.
A deformed face
without a nose
deprived of eyes
but blessed
by the gods
with a big
goofy
mouth.

Sunk

I lock myself inside my room
and stare at the moon
but the black raven
is gurgling in the wood
mourning my wistful childhood.
The voice gets louder
and the roof seems closer.
I try to overcome my fear
but a thorny hand pulls me
deeper and deeper
into a dark well
where the echoes
of dead flowers float
through my skin as they sing:
"You love and love and love
then you die slow "

Homo Sapiens aka the wise ass

In the beginning
Man created the gods
then killed them.
And discovered the lands
then destroyed them.
And sailed the oceans
then defiled them.
And invented the machines
then misused them.
And domesticated the animals
then slaughtered them.
At the end
Man socialized with other men
then enslaved them.

Sexy nine

The year '69
was unique
in many ways:
Pop culture
Politics
Science
The Beatles
Woodstock
Charles Manson
Apollo 11
Boeing 747
Etc....

But our 69
was different.
My 6 was hard
and salty.
Her 9 was tight
and juicy.
She wiped her mouth

and said,
"You're a perfect mess,
Omar."
I looked at her
upside down,
"I'm the universe,
sweetie,
and you're
my falling star."

Interrupted conversation

Under a dim light
in the middle
of a dark room
my shadow sat
in front of me, legs crossed
a cigar in his mouth
staring at me
at this empty gloomy figure.
"Life is a short walk." he said.
"Book your seat and enjoy the trip."
"I'm like an aborted fetus."
I answered the shadow.
"My journey has ended
before it even gets started."
Then there was a silence
inside the room.
He was studying my gestures
and deciphering my thoughts
when my wife opened up the door.
A glimpse of light hit my tired eyes.

"Hey darlin', you ok?"
Her voice echoed
deep in my eardrum
then made it's way
to my guts and half turned
back to my throat,
lifted up my tongue
and opened up my mouth.
"'I'm ok." I murmured.
"Come on, pumpkin,
my tits feel lonely tonight." she said.
Then once again
her words broke
like a glowing arrow
and went straight
to my cold heart
'till I felt a sting in my cock.
"Yes honey, let's fuck." I said
and I left the room.
Before I closed the door,
I took another glance
just to make sure
my shadow, this time,
is not following me.

Love gun

She has a nice butt
and a weird mind.
She studies astrology
and writes poetry.
She takes dope
and hates the Pope.
She chews gum
and carries a gun.
I said, "Hey babe,
do you love me?"
She said, "idk, maybe."
I wanted to ask again,
but she shot out my brain.
She took a paper and a pen
and wrote a bloody note
"To whom it may concern
you've got a lesson to learn...
I have never fucking loved any man
and next time's gonna be your turn."

Unwelcome visitor

Dear death,
What you smell is
just a deflection of
your burning fears
and what you see is
just a blurry reflection of
my pure soul in
the sea of
your deep
defeat.

Lullaby

And when you snore
the angry gods
illuminate the dark sky
with the big bright moon,
like a flashlight
in their hands
to pursue
the melodious tone
that aroused
their babe stars
and made them dance
in the middle of a peaceful night.

Waiting in vain

Here I am
building a temple
for my holy solitude
and waiting
for the sunshine
to fade away
and the darkness
to light my way.

Here I am
waiting
but in vain.

Waiting
still
but it feels like
waiting
under the rain
for the rainbow
to heal your pain.

Go mad

Do not be afraid of
going mad.
Madness is rather
an artistic metaphor of
the noblest
and highest
manifestation of
the human consciousness.
Live like mad and
die like mad
and between this and that
love like mad.

Listen to me

I often run conversations
with my shadow, my shoes,
my books, the walls, the fly,
the spider...etc.
and those conversations
just remind me how lonely
one can be.
How lonely a wall,
a fly, a spider, a pair of shoes,
or even a book with its thousands words
can be.
Call it schizophrenia
or delusional disorder,
or PTSD or just BS.
I call it the subtle art
of listening to the mellow
tone of madness.

Dream lovers

After a few drinks
I kissed her warm lips
and we felt like two souls
caged in our dark dreams.
She said, "I miss you dear
like the birds miss
the early morning breeze."
I said, "Meet me in the dark
side of the moon tonight."
She said, " I'm a dead flower
blooming only after midnight.
Wrap me in your arms
and feed me with the nectar
of your bleeding heart."
"Lay your head", I said,
"On the pillow of my pride
and sleep babe sleep
'till the end like a child."

Sniff

Everything smells good
with the right people
at the right time
in the right place.
Your morning coffee
smells good.
The late evening wind
smells good.
Your cheap wine
smells good.
Even when you vomit,
it still smells good.
Your rotten soul
smells good.
Even when you ruin
my life,
it still smells good.
So come on babe,
let's take a shower
and play with water
'till it smells of love.

Unadorned hearts

I'm not a fan of sunsets
nor the whistle of birds.
The morning sunshine
makes me feel blue and
most of the time lonely.
I hate Friday evening parties
and the stupid people
with fancy, shiny shoes too.
I love you, but the thing is
I would rather invite you
for a drink and light
the cigarette in your mouth
than to send you a flower
on Valentine's Day.
So how's that?
Oh babe! I love you too!
Let's drink more wine
and please hon,
keep in your mind
that you're the Zippo
to my cigarette heart.

Daliesque

When the sky darkened
and the stars fell into
a tenebrous night
I wrecked into the sea
of your crystal tears
where the midnight sun
missed your naked back
and the castle of sand
missed your wet footprints

Nocturnes

I turn my phonograph on
and let play the Nocturnes.
Abandoned, my thoughts get lost in the vast dark
isthmus.
I look at the mirror and stare at this pale face
in front of me.
Ironically I wonder:
Who I am?
Two dry lips like an arid desert land.
Who I am?
The mouth is a dark cave and the teeth are like
stalactite.
Who I am?
My nose looks like a steam train tunnel.
Who I am?
Two sleeping eyes, almost bursting with blood.
Who I am?
Shaggy hair like a cloud of black smoke.
Who I am?
Tell me. Oh you think you know me right?
I will tell you.
I am you and what I see is me.

Renault 4 blues

Alone I drive my little Renault car
crossing the narrow streets of the city old
town.
Still and lost in my thoughts
hands on the steering wheel,
eyes staring at the rear mirror of my life.
The blurry lights beyond the window dance
in my head, worms eating my brain.
Camel Wide hanging from my lips
a loose black necktie,
a worn out white shirt,
thunder rustles in the pale sky.
Despite this
a soft voice in my car sings:
"And I think to myself what a wonderful
world."

Human, all too human

When you see a blind man
led by his guide dog
be grateful to the Lord
for the grace of being and seeing.
That's what they will teach you, son.
Now listen to me.
When you see a blind man
led by his guard dog
be grateful that dogs exist.
Be more grateful that one dog
is more human than all humans.
More human than all the gods.

I'm hungry

I'm hungry and want to eat.
I want a beautiful girl to serve me and smile at
me, and smile at her back.
I'm hungry and want to eat.
But, I don't want to talk to a machine.
I don't want a machine to take my order or
give me orders.
I'm a human and I need to eat.
I'm human and I need a human to listen to me.
To serve me and thank me with spoken words.
I'm human. And hungry.
I'm human. And angry.
Fuck algorithms.

Love, sex, and poetry in Sevilla

We stood in the middle
of la Plaza de España
unconcerned by the laughing dove
over our heads.
We kissed
deep, and
sunk
in an eternal silence.
Then we hugged
and felt the beats of our hearts
mingle with the Sevillanas guitar
and the Olé shouts in the air.

"You are love
itself," she said,
"walking through
the old town streets
of Sevilla
like a gypsy clown
shooting flowers."

"If I ever make love to you,"
I said,
"while looking at
your sleepy eyes,
I would come, very fast,
with a load of poems
and shoot off
ineffaceable words
on your innocent face."

.

Lust in exile

When you and I
make love
the doors of heaven shut
and the filthy demons
get released
from the kingdom of
forbidden lust.

Madness

Sometimes
madness comes
to you
with
a soul
and even
a body
like a quiet woman
with a wicked smile.

Natural born drunk

She is drunk when she makes love
drunk when she dances
barefoot.
She is drunk when she breaks hearts
drunk when she cries
at night.
She is drunk when she makes promises
drunk when she sleeps
and snores.
She is drunk when she combs her hair
drunk when she swims
naked.
She is drunk when she drives her car
drunk when she yawns
and moans.
She is drunk when she walks and talks.
She is drunk all day long
but never drunk
when she drinks.
Ever.

Submit

Death is a greedy hand
wrinkled and cold
that never gets tired
of stealing lives
innocent and damned alike.
So write down your name here
and submit your story while you pour
whiskey into your lonely soul,
and blaze like an angry volcano.
After all
no one would dare to steal
a piece of blank, burned paper.

Cirque

Life! This carnival of laughers and gamblers
where the sun never ceases to rise, and it rises
often the same.
A vicious cycle where the seconds become
minutes.
Minutes after minutes till the last minute.
Always easier to count minutes than to wait
for hours.
24 hours, like a herd of turtles, crawling to the
edge of the day.
The days were given names like the gods,
and like the gods, they move slow, although
they are few.
Sometimes they make love to one another
and give birth to unknown weeks,
then the weeks grow up to months
and the months age to years and the years
carry the pain.
And then pain becomes immortal.
You laugh at it.

Then one day you drink enough
to get some courage to say 'Enough!'
You laugh and like a gambler
you forsake your life
for a gentle death.

Words, roses, and scars

The words from
her mouth came
like a company of
soldiers with bayonets
attacking my
unarmed gentleness.
The knives tore
my body and soul
and my eyes shed tears
that dropped onto
my solid feet
like a heavy rain
of bombs
and burst into
tons of thorned roses.

Just listen

Of all the artists, dead and alive,
Nature is indeed, the more creative
and most talented.
Early sunrises and late sunsets
dewy nights and brand new days
blue skies and green fields
bright lightnings and soft winds
billions of galaxies and dark oceans.
A spontaneous and wild art
that dazzles the mind
and nourishes the soul.
Yet, the nature's masterpiece
is the immortal silence.
Listen.

I am a serial killer

I am a serial killer
and I can't remember
how many passing dreams
I have killed?
How many stray ideas
I have strangled?
With my cold typewriter
during my most
distressful solitude
with the same
Modus Operandi
and the unique
signature.

I stalk my victims
and chase them
like a dreamcatcher.
Hair raising thoughts
smiling at me
waiting for me

men
women
perverts
whores
hitchhikers
bankers
dancing their way up
to heaven
but I catch them
red handed
and lock them up
inside the cells of
my deranged mind
till they start
to decompose
to small syllables
and scatter
to malformed letters
just like body parts
found in an
abandoned bunker.

H for the head

upside down
on the sofa
A for arms
crossed
under the table
B for blood
fresh
on the wall
E for eyes
rolling
down the stairs,
T for tongue
crawling
like a severed snake.

I am a serial killer
and nothing satisfies
my caprice
more than watching
a new born idea
slowly dying
between my fingers.

Futile prayer

Allahu Akbar
shouts in the air
Sunday churches
and wailers at the wall.

Temples and fingers crossed
prayers here and there
from dawn to dusk.
Holy books read
every then and now.

Dear God,
Isn't it time to swallow your pride
and listen to those defeated souls?
Their prayers, I swear
are just a humble cry
begging your Holiness
to correct your divine mistakes.

Drunken love

I wish I could dance
with my demons
in the hell of your mind
or sink foolishly
like a silver dime
in the sea of your red blood,
or get blown away like a feather
to the end of nowhere
by the hurricane of your breath
or just lay under your eyes
while you cry
and get drunk with the wine
of your sweetened tears.

Dirty blue jeans

Hush
lil' babe!
I'm here
for you
with you
wherever
you go.
Under your skin
through your veins
and inside
the ripped pockets
of your dirty
blue jeans.

A fool such as I

Like cotton candy
my hands carry
her madness.

Like a golden saxophone
my fingers tease
her nipples.

Like a soft egg
my palms warm
her heart's nest.

And like a fool
I gave her my heart
but she only
wanted my arms.

The moon

The moon
is a nuthouse
where the poet
the drunk
and the dreamer
end up
while seeking
the beauty
behind the silent night
and the mystery
of the dark rainy sky.

Junkie

When I overdose
on music
love
and sex
I just wish
I could
dance on
the melody of
your moan
till I have a
heart attack and
fall at your feet
dead
with a hard on
and flipping everyone off.

Bullfighting

Our love was nothing but a corrida
where my heart was the bleeding bull
and you were the skillful matador
who knew how to stab and when
with words sharper than swords.

The People Look Like Flowers at Last

So we left the 3 for 2
bookshop.
It was 4 p.m.
and the rays of sun
burst through the cloudy
sky of Oslo.
We put on our sunglasses
and held each other's hands.
We walked by the glass facade shops
of jewelry
and luxury goods.
There was a reflection
of my bearded face
and shaggy hair.
In front of us
there was a beautiful blonde couple
wearing fashionable clothes
and fancy shoes,
walking a mouse shaped dog.

We stopped at Pascal,
a bakery a la francaise,
and came in to buy 2 cakes.
She picked up a small yellow cake
and I asked if there is any
with chocolate.
For me, cakes are chocolate
and chocolate is all I know.
" Bien sure", said Pascal,
a tall clean shaven man
and he continued:
"This one is very good,
it is made with vanilla from Madagascar."
"Madagascar!" I nodded. "Yeah okay."
I don't know why
but at that moment
I thought about
a poetry collection of Bukowski
I saw earlier at the bookstore
called The People Look Like Flowers at Last.
Well!
Sometimes,
you just have to eat French cakes

and keep your mouth shut.
I mean shut not to let the the Madagascar
vanilla flavor fade away.

In the name of the bottle

I drink, wandering through
the green grasslands
in the flowering spring evenings
enchanted with the laughter
of children on the muddy valley bank.

I drink and pray to the gods
of the moon and nights
when the demons of the blue sky
pull the curtains down and the birds
sing the sad sunset anthem.

I drink when the shooting stars awake
and when the drunk mermaids
join the show and dance under
the vintage wine of dew, falling
on my nose like the first snow
of a lonely Christmas night.

A résumé

I am a walking
madness.
I inhale love
and exhale
death.
At times I drink
from the poisoned
well of words
and shit my
own sanity
out.

Homage

I sailed on Rimbaud's boat
and crossed Cousteau's deep oceans
along with Chopin's Nocturnes
while drinking the Havana Club rum
and singing Ode To Joy
until I reached Vincent's folly.
Then the thrill was gone
and I was left empty
like Mason's drums.

Foot in mouth

She has dirty feet
and I have a toothless mouth.

We drink everyday
and eat every
second day.

We have one bed
and billions of dreams.

We make love instead
of making money,
and we feed cats instead
of feeding our ambitions.

"One day my dear,
I will honour your feet
with sexy high heels"
I told her.

Then we hugged
in front of the shoe shop
window.

It reflected my happy
toothless mouth
and it looked more charming
than a host's smile.

Bukowski

It is never too late
to become the
masterpiece you
have worked on
your whole life.

And remember
your life is nothing
but a bunch of
unfinished drafts
of poems, novels,
and short stories,
you wrote every day
after midnight
while pouring scotch
and beer, mostly beer
on the blue bird
inside your heart.

And either you drink

until age of 74
or end up in a coffin
before that
make sure
to tear the
papers off
and never look back
at your past.

Never make decisions
(serious ones)
while sober.
The only thing
you are allowed
to do while sober
is to sleep.

So sleep long,
dear Hank.

Sleep, because
ain't so much
going on nowadays.

The beer doesn't
taste like beer
any more
the naked legs
won't attract you
like they used to do.
And people are busy
with their smartphones
and they have no time
to read your ornate truth.

Sadist

I make love to her
then I walk away
hands in pockets
whistling
and let her rot
in the hell of remorse.
She begs
but I ignore her cry
and put more salt
on the bloody steak.
I eat
and watch her drowning
in the stream of tears.
"Help me! Help me!"
The sound echoes from
the depth
but I drink and raise my cup
"Hail to death!",
and she dies.
I have never loved
her,
my solitude.

Lady of the night

I fell in love
with a smiling flower
I can't sleep anymore.
O, lady of the night
you're dear to my heart.
I fell in love
she's tall 'n' hot
chews gum, drinks 'n' smokes.
O, lady of the night
you're dear to my heart.
I fell in love
Mona Lisa of the streets
and bars, Venus of backseats.
O, lady of the night
you're dear to my heart.
I fell in love
but mom said, "No way!"
Dad said, "What's wrong with ya son!"
O, lady of the night
you're dear to my heart.

I fell in love
do you love me?
You, mother of the day,
hooker of the night?

Deprived

At the age
of 33
I became
Anosmic
&
Ageusiatic.
What a loss!
When I can't
even smell
the scent
of our stinky bed
and taste from
the wild fruit
of our lusty love.
Oh what a shame!
At that young age
you become
smell-less
taste-less.
Meaningless.

Companions

Dear loners,
I have 2 skilled demons for sale.
Male & female.
Drummers and nerve dancers.
Immortal.
Night shift only.
Accepted rewards:
Music, hash, and whiskey.
PS: They have an allergy
for stupidity.
Delivery:
By the time
you finish
reading this
they will
already be
somewhere
in your left brain
telling jokes
and laughing.
You've been hacked.
Smile.

Birthday dream

On a cold winter day
I saw the early morning sun rise
and the rays burst through the blue sky.
I asked myself
"Am I dreaming?"
So I walked to the garden.
To my surprise
I saw a bouquet of
white lilies
and 2 blue jays whistling
a German waltz.
It wasn't until my alarm rang
that I opened my eyes
you by my side
with a dim light sneaking
out from the kitchen.
And when I looked around
there was no sun
but your warm smile
and no blue sky

but your sparkling iris
and no birds
but the smell of your messy hair
and no flowers,
but a note under your pillow
with Happy Birthday wishes,
a smile,
and a heart.

The lie of Spring

Here comes Spring
upon the wet grass
swaying slightly
on its flowery feet
and the sun awakens
on the sound of the
whispering trees
and the birds floating
in the vast blue.
It is life.
But a miserable one
without depth,
without meaning.
I swear on the name
of your skinny ankles
that I long for our
endless winter nights
when your nakedness
covered up my shivering bones
and when your brightness

lightened up my dark dreams
and when your silliness
broke down my boring life
and when your naughtiness
rearranged my devouted mind.
I long for your craziness
'cause it reminds me that,
sometimes, happiness
is nothing but a drunk wo-
man with a closed-lip smile.

Constant gardener

I am a wild garden
at the top of the
Atlas mountains.
My thoughts grow
inside my mind
and through my guts.
I need to quench
them with whiskey,
wine, rum & beer
(Vodka sometimes).
I inhale smoke
to kill the parasites
and use chemicals
to fertilize the seeds.
Otherwise I will dry up
and like the Greek ruins
left to die.

The roots of evil

The history of mankind
is divided between
those who kill and
those who condemn.
Every time
a massacre is committed
in the name of a man,
an idea, or a god,
and every time
we hear the same chorus:
"It's not us...it doesn't represent us."
Stop this shit.
The evil is rooted
in our outdated scriptures,
and dripping from our leaders' tongues.
Kill the savage gods
and impeach the
fascism megaphones
with orange wigs and red ties.

A hygienic advice

What is love?
Love is the dirt
under the nails,
the white hair
in the nose,
and the wax
inside the ear.
Nasty
but
necessary.
So
clean,
trim,
&
wipe
carefully.

Vagabond worm

Come little babe,
there is a tree growing
inside my heart
and the birds are eating
from the grains of my mind.
Take my eyes away
let the branches come out.
Lie down under the shades
and sow seeds beneath my feet
for I am neither dead nor alive
but a vagabond worm
stuck between the now and then.

Let me fly

The plane has always
been a mystery to me.
This feeling has continued
until the age of 30
when, on one winter day,
I flew for the first time in my life:
Destination Istanbul.
And here I am
my feet standing on the runway
facing this white, giant, metal machine.
The strange thing is that
(as I recall)
I was attracted by the shape
of its huge sleek tires
and it really tickled my feelings.
But this feeling soon faded away
as my flights continued
only to be replaced
by an innocent wonder
about the secret behind

the non-stop smiling face
of the hostesses.
It must be the magic of flying
for many hours in the sky
and through the clouds
far way from this rotten earth.
It's the purity of the universe.
Now I will reveal the reasons
why I am a non-believer:
Demons do not inhabit heaven
as we have been told by the holy books.
I haven't seen any there.
I have seen beautiful young girls
with fine legs, and good looking gentlemen
with strong arms.
All of them, smiling.
All the time.
Real demons live between us
and share the air we breathe.
Down there.
And beside that,
when you are 10 km up in the air space,
your only God, who truly holds your fate,

is the captain inside his cabin.

So keep quiet babe
and pray he had a nice day
with his wife.
Otherwise,
your life jacket is just under your ass.

Spring

O, spring of my winter
may all the gloomy faces smile
and all the dark souls shine.
O, spring of my winter
may all the bottles get
uncorked for the late evening parties
and all the bathrooms get
cleaned for the early morning pukes.
O, spring of my winter
may all your wives stay young
and all your husbands remain faithful.
O, spring of my winter
may the love gardens bloom dildos
and the blue sky rain tits.
O, spring of my winter
may all the loners find peace
and all the haters sink deep.

Legacy

His name was G.
He was in his 40's
with no job, no family,
and his hobby was to wander
the streets of my hometown,
begging for food and singing
folk music in front of
the cafes' terraces.
What nobody knew about G.
is that he had another hobby:
To shit on the streets,
on car hoods, and
at the doorsteps of my office.
He was a poor guy
who believed that his duty as
a deprived human being was
to share his music
and crap with us.
It wasn't until lately,
when an old woman reported

to the police that G.
was found dead after
he fell into her well.
This news left all the community
in shock,
but at least it unveiled one of
the city's biggest mysteries.
Now that G. is gone,
the streets,
car hoods,
my office doorsteps,
are left shitless.
People come and go.
Some are good and
most are just good
at pissing you off.
Some leave organic shit,
fresh.
And some throw shit on you
from their mouths and,
believe me, it smells
even nastier than
the real shit coming

right from the rectum.
Rest in peace.

The drunk cabaret

You are my lost muse
my lucky fool
the cabaret of my escape.
You light the cigarette
of my lust
with the fire of your lips.
And inhale the smoke
of my thoughts
with the rays of your eyes.
While you drink the wine
of my patience
with the beats of your heart.

Do you?

I don't know
if you get this
feeling sometimes
when you decide
to turn your TV on,
just like in the old days,
and suddenly you see
respectful ladies and gentlemen
gathered around a table
with a nice background design.
The elegant broadcaster
with his artificial smile
who races against the time
to meet his mistress.
Then there is the Dr. X
who understands everything,
and doesn't like anything.
The bohemian with thick hair
and exotic glasses. A red scarf too.
Finally, there is the lady wearing

a black open chest dress to disguise
her tacky style.
All of them talking about
literature, art, creativity, and pain
with their sophisticated
tongues and gestures,
and expensive shoes and watches...
lipstick and trimmed eyebrows...
they have a lot to show
but little to give.
Then I think about Choukri,
Celine, Rimbaud, Sylvia,
Buk, Crane, Ernie, Vincent,
Sexton, Syd, De Sade, Mishima...
People who had little to show
but a lot to give:
Simplicity.
Authenticity.
Honesty.
And madness.
By the time I finished writing this,
the show came to the end.
I turned the TV off,

played Tom Waits' Small Change,
and picked up a book,
The Flowers of Evil.

126

M for Mad

M for the moon
say the poets.
M for magic
say the lovers.
M for Mona Lisa
say the artists.
M for madness
says the silly.
M for me.
I say:
M ay you stay forever mad,
A nd sweet like
D ates.

On the road

On the road I walk
my head held high
my feet on the ground
across the mirage.
On the road
I walk, or rather,
I race against time
on the path of hope
without a rucksack
but with heavy dreams
on my back.
On the road
I walk, I jog,
I run, I fly, I swim
in the airspace
above the clouds.
With the gods
I sing and drink.
With the shining
sun I dance.

Then I dissolve
and fall apart,
like rain drops
like the dew
on the wasteland
of the south
of no present.
The present
of no south.

Poet's Day

Focus
and write a
new poem
'cause today is
World Poetry Day!
It doesn't matter.
Write poetry or prose
free verse or rhyme.
A one-night-stand fuck-ink.
BS has become
a registered trademark.
Use ambiguous words
and don't try to make sense.
Abstraction is the criteria
for successful artwork.
You are allowed to lie.
You are a writer
after all.
Hurry up!
Your followers

on social media
are waiting
in their cozy nests
like baby birds
(naked &
eyes closed)
for the worms.
Write babe write!
Scholars, critics,
and intellectuals
are sharpening
their venomous tongues
ready to execute
the innocent art
in the name of
your mediocrity
at public squares
whilst the angry
people gather around
the guillotine
yelling,
"Death to the
damned poet!"

Pain in my ass

Okay, this is not a poem.
This is just a fun story
I would love to share with you.
Yesterday
while I was sitting
in my garden, counting the stars
and trying hard to find my muse
a bottle of wine by my side
my phone buzzed.
A new message received.
One of my fb friends wrote:
"Your poetry
is very
depressing.
I know you've
had mental disorders...
Stop reading Bukowski...
it won't help you.
Have a nice day."
"Thank you my dear friend."

I answered her.
Then I continued
"What is an artist without pain?
Pain is like the typewriter for the poet
like the brush for the painter
like the instruments for the musician
like the stage for the actor.
Without pain
an artist is like a drunk monkey.
I don't claim to be an artist
but like all artists
I feel the pain too, deep inside me.
Not in my heart or soul though,
but somewhere else...
And you are the pain in my ass.
xxx."

The blind architect

Life, at its best, is a stage
and at its worst is a zoo.
Where the honest artist
performs his role faithfully
and the wild animal behaves
according to its instinct.
Both with a common denominator:
Spontaneity.
You will also find
the fawning artist
performing his role
only to satisfy this and that
and you will find the greedy animal
always asking for more.
Both with a common denominator:
Arrogance.
And there is the futile artist
who can do everything except act
and there is the house trained animal
which its actions reflect a developed

evolution.

With only one difference that separates the
former from the latter:

The bars.

Finally, there are the spectators.

Whether in the theater or in the zoo,

they enjoy their time

while eating popcorn

and drinking coke.

Either a human or an animal

for them it's the same.

You play your role

you get paid, and that's all.

Sorry, I didn't introduce myself.

I am the one who built

the theater and the zoo

and the one who sells

the tickets too.

I am the one.

The architect

of

contradictions.

Piano of my life

Inside my room
between the four
imaginary walls
I write the lyrics
for my new song.
You are magic
and magic is
the piano of my life.
Small world
messy room.
Wide world
a mighty illusion.
Words rhyme
with words.
The piano invades
my soul
like Napoleon's army.
But where are you?
Your mother died
your father's dating

a young prostitute,
your brother's a junkie
and your sister's on
her honeymoon
in southern Italy.
The moon is high
the piano is drunk
the words are silent
and I long for you.
Sweet love
of mine
my sunshine.
I miss you
all the time.

For bread alone

"Years
of emotional drought,
spiritual poverty,
imaginary hope.
Existential voyage,
in search of love
and knowledge.
In search of
myself..."

Some reflections
popped into my mind
while I was sitting
in the cafe
watching the passersby
and cars.
I follow their movements
mechanically
like a spectator
at a tennis match.

I smoke a cigarette
and drink coffee.
Then
a shadow appeared
from nowhere
as he walked with
heavy steps.
Long hair.
Ripped trainers.
Shit and urine spots
on his jeans.
He had a loaf of bread
and a tail-cut dog
behind him.
He sat on
the pavement and
shared the bread
with the dog.
What about me?
You?
Us?
Sitting there in the cafe
like pseudo-intellectuals

(zombies).
We ask questions
that do not exist
and seek useless
answers.
Just so you know
my friends,
that for people
like him,
we don't think.
We don't pretend.
Nope!
We piss.
We shit.
We love animals.
And we share
a loaf of
bread.

Fetish

I was lost,
studying her gestures.
I felt like...Kafka's Gregor Samsa.
Not an insect though
but a puppy
sticking out his tongue
wagging his tail
waiting for the bone
to lick.
And her goddamn fine legs
looked just like a fresh bone.
"Hey buddy? You ok?"
she asked.
"Yeah!
I was just thinking
about the unthinkable.
The futility of fate.
I am a poet.
Ya know!
I dream more than I breathe

and I'm a better sculptor
with words
than with syntax."
"Okay! What's your name?"
she asked
while puffing on a fag.
"Legman", I said.
"My name is Silly O. Legman."
"Are you a believer Mr Legman?"
she asked.
"No.
But you can be my goddess
if you don't mind."
I said.
"Really?"
She put out her cig
and took a sip of her scotch.
I looked at her
lipstick-stained glass
then at her fox- like eyes.
"I swear by your
white ankles
that you are."

"You're naughty."
she said.
"No, I am a filthy hermit.
I worship your arched feet
and the secret of my faith
lies under your black high heels."
She smiled
and put on her sunglasses
kissed my cheek
and whispered in my ear
"Sorry baby, gotta run.
My old man is waiting
in the car outside.
Ciao."
She left.
I ordered another beer
and opened my book.
I don't remember which chapter it was
but it started like this:
"It is, after all, not necessary to fly right into
the middle of the sun, but it is necessary to
crawl to a clean little spot on Earth where the
sun sometimes shines and one can warm
oneself a little."
Cheers.

A conversation at 3 a.m.

It was a short message:
"What do you want from me?"
I sat by my laptop and wrote an answer:
"Babe, I
want you.
I want
your love,
your heart
your soul,
your flesh
your blood
your mind
your life
your demons
and angels.
I want you
naked as
a mermaid
swimming in
the pool

of our love
while I play
the violin
with your
wet hair
and eat
the peaches
of your ripe breasts"
I glanced at the screen
for 5 or 10 seconds,
then I took
a deep breath
and laughed.
I deleted my answer
and wrote a new one:
"nothing".
This time
the message
was sent.
And I didn't laugh.
I turned the lights off
and went to bed.

Threesome

Drunk with
the scent
of jasmine air
a soft hand wrapped me
in my flowery bed
while two gentle doves
hovered around my head
one named Paloma
and the other Colomba.
They sat on my bare chest
playing with my tight nipples.
They said,
"Come with us!
Let's fly and swim
naked in the vast blue sky."
Oh my dear
how I wish
I could fly.
How I wish
I were a dove

to hover high
and one day
share my florid bed
with you
and pray to the gods
to forgive our sins
and have mercy on us.

Stolen waters are sweet

At first
she smiled to me.
I felt the excitement
boil in my veins
like a bull fighter.
I took the risk
and jumped naked
in the sea of
forbidden love
and swam
to a remote island
where only the moon
and the bright stars
could witness
the marriage of
our sins.
Early in the morning
lying under a tall palm tree
awakened by
the sound of the waves

and the hovering gulls
her silence spoke to me
"I can't" she said
with unspoken words.
Then a sharp tear
wounded her soft cheek.
With the burden
of sorrow and shame
my eyes narrowed
my heart tightened
and I prayed to the gods
to curse my sinful soul
and turn me into
a rain drop
to fall on her
caramel body
and wash off
the dust of our
sweet sins.

The western wind

I promise you
my love
that I will be waiting
for the western wind
to blow
to take my kiss away
and put it on your lips.

And If the western wind
misses the way to your lips
then I will get myself
a bottle of wine and
drink until the middle of the night
and when the moon is full
I will howl like a wolf and tear my heart away
from my bare chest
and lock it inside
the bottle
and throw it
from the top of the mountain

and watch it sailing
through
the darkest seas and
the deepest oceans
to the shore of your wet mouth.

Socks of my heart

She wears me
like a pair of socks
and makes me dirty
like a pair of socks.

She washes my sins
like a pair of socks
and dries my wetness
like a pair of socks.

Her heart cages my soul
like a pair of socks
cages my feet.

Alas!
My dear friends!

What is a foot
without a warm
pair of socks

in winter time?

And what is a soul
without a warm heart
in lonely times?

Warm me, dear socks of my feet.
Love me, sweet heart of my soul.

Endorphin

We were both
sitting on the sofa.
Wasn't too much going on that day.
I had a quarrel with my boss
she had her period
and a don't-fuck-with-me face.

TV was on
a young doctor talking about
endorphin.

Endorphin!
Foolishly I asked "What's that, babe?"
She didn't look at me.
She picked up her Marlboro,
lit a cigarette, took a puff
and passed it to me
"This is endorphin, fucker."

She didn't look at me.

She took a sip of wine
and passed the glass to me,
"This is endorphin."
She didn't curse this time
but still without looking at me.

Then she spread her legs
and showed off her
blood-stained pussy
and slapped it gently,
"real endorphin shit is right here.
Let's get you some,
my sweet pumpkin!"

And this time she looked at me
with a big smile on her face.

Yes, easy as brain surgery

Unlike politics
art simplifies
the complex.

Decomposes
the compound.

And prettifies
the dirt.

Be simple
authentic
honest
and mad
at the same time
then you will
create art.

Easy?
Isn't it?

Snake of love

I crawl around
your smooth naked back
like a snake crawls
around a peachtree
enchanted by the scent
of your swan neck
and the delicate aroma
of your hair.

Swallowing the nectar
dripping from your armpits
my venom turns into a holy water
and my sharp tongue
into a slender hand.
The magic of your eyes
turns the deadly snake
into a blessed saint
ready to baptize
(In the name of love, lust, and holy desire)
your pierced nipples.

Hope

Stop crying
my friend.
One day
the dogs will
run away from
your dreams
and howl at dawn
forthright throughout the day
and when the night comes
the dogs won't return
and you will sleep
for too long
like never before.

Acknowledgements

I would love to express my special thanks to my friend and editor B.T.M., as well as my Facebook friends for their support and encouragement. Without them, this book would not exist and would not have found its way into your hands.

"I started out with nothing and I still got most
of it left."

-Tom Waits